How Would Jesus Vote?

AN IN-DEPTH LOOK AT THE BIBLE'S VIEW
CONCERNING TODAY'S HOT POLITICAL ISSUES

by

The KingdomHasCome, LLC

How Would Jesus Vote?

Copyright © 2004
The KingdomHasCome, LLC

ISBN: 0-9761918-0-6 (previously ISBN: 1-4120-3754-9)

Scripture quotations are taken from THE HOLY BIBLE, *King James Version*, or unless otherwise noted.

Cover design by the Broken Chains Design Group, Inc.

Printed in the United States of America

10   9   8   7   6   5   4   3   2   1

— Table of Contents —

— Dedication —

*We dedicate this book to our wonderful Father
God, our Lord and Savior Jesus Christ, and
our Senior Partner, the Holy Ghost, whose
desire is that all men be saved and come into
the knowledge of the truth.*

*"Not as though I had already attained,
either were already perfect: but I follow
after, if that I may apprehend that
for which also I am apprehended
of Christ Jesus."*

Philippians 3:12

Introduction

"He that saith he abideth in him ought himself also so to walk, even as he walked."
1 John 2:6

I f Jesus were a United States citizen, having all the legal rights and responsibilities of voting, according to what standards would He vote? Seeing that God's Word teaches that we should live as He lived, and walk as He walked, this becomes an important question for today's Christian.

Recently, God birthed a revelation into the Body of Christ that has spread in the form of a simple question. Men, women, boys, and girls faced with life's situations are learning to ask: What would Jesus do?

Although recognized in some circles as a trend or fad, this question is one that every Christian should ask in every situation because, when properly addressed, this question sets the pattern for their lifestyle.

What *would* Jesus do? Even the Apostle Paul saw the importance of this question when writing to the church at

Philippi. His admonishment was not that they look to him as their sole example of how to live, but he encouraged them to look to the One he served—Jesus Christ.

For Paul, Jesus was the example. And so it should be with us as Christians.

How Would Jesus Vote Today?

This is a challenging concept, as most people have already adopted certain standards by which they vote. Some vote strictly according to race, while others select their candidates based on personal beliefs. If he's a Christian, he's the right man for the job. If she believes like I do, she must be right.

Still, others look to see how a candidate stands on the financial issues. What will they do about the economy? Will they raise taxes? Improve our streets and highways? What about Medicare and Medicaid?

These are all good questions and represent important issues. But my friends, they are not reasons for selecting the people or persons who will ultimately make the decisions that may affect you for the rest of your life.

When you are facing important decisions such as voting, finances should never be the deciding factor. Decisions at the poll should never be dictated by what is good for your pockets. They should always be directed by what is right. Do you remember what the Bible said about the love of money?

"For the love of money is the root of all evil..."
(1 Timothy 6:10).

The Bible provides a very basic, fundamental principle concerning life for the body of Christ, and that is that we are to live by every word of God.

"And Jesus answered him, saying, It is written, That man shall not live by bread alone, but by every word of God" (Luke 4:4).

The Word of God, the Bible, should act as final authority in every area of our lives. This applies to our family, our finances, and our professions. Even our political affiliations are dictated by what the Bible says.

The Bible is our manual for living. When we are confronted with ideals or beliefs that contradict what the Bible has to say, then we are to choose God's Word over what anything or anyone else says.

A Revealed Principle

Jesus understood this principle. He was not just quoting a scripture when He said that man is to live by every word of God. He was revealing to us *how He lived.*

In John 8:29, Jesus said, *"I do always those things that please him (God)."* This is further illustrated by what God said concerning Jesus when He was about thirty years old and about to enter the ministry. God said that He was well-pleased with Jesus (Mark 1:11), but notice that God's pleasure was not based on the miracles Jesus performed like healing the sick, raising the dead, or casting out devils. It was not even based on the fact that Jesus went to the cross and died for the sins of mankind. None of these things had happened yet.

God was well pleased because Jesus took the time to find out what God's Word said about every situation before He would deal with it. In every area of life, no matter what it involved, no matter what the circumstances were, Jesus looked to God and His Word for direction. He lived His life according to God's ideals and beliefs. He governed every ounce of His decision-making based on what God had to say. And because of that, Jesus was without sin. That is how we, as Christians, are to live.

How would Jesus vote today? The answer is simple. First, He would seek God.

As Christians, we have a responsibility to make sure that God's will is manifested in this country. Believe it or not, what happens in our society is not entirely dependent on the politicians, the media, or the maneuvering of those who stand against the things of God. In the Old Testament, God told Israel that if HIS people, those who were called by His name, would seek His face, He would heal their land (2 Chronicles 7:14). This principle still holds true today, showing that God is the same God today as He was then.

> *"Jesus Christ the same yesterday, and today, and forever" (Hebrews 13:8).*

The disastrous things we see taking place in our society today—disease, famine, terrorism, and war—are happening partly because the church of the Lord Jesus Christ is allowing them to happen. As a whole, Christians have chosen to sit outside the political arena. They either believe the lie that "God has everything in control, so I don't need to do anything," or they buy into the political rhetoric falsely espoused under the name of "separation of church and state" that there is no place for God and His values in our government—a belief that continues to prove more and more devastating to our country as Satan has been given free rein to kill, steal, and destroy.

Until the body of Christ rises up and takes its rightful place and exercises its authority—a place and authority God has clearly established—this nation will continue to spiral downward on the path of destruction on which it is currently headed.

How do we take our place? First, we pray as God's Word has instructed us to do. Then, we exercise our God-given right and duty to vote; not according to the standards and dictates of man, but according to God's Word. We follow the example set by Jesus and allow God's Word to be final authority over the word of man.

Now that we have established what our approach should be toward voting, let's look at ten of today's major issues and see how Jesus would respond to them at the voting polls.

*"BEFORE I formed thee in the belly I knew
thee; and BEFORE thou camest forth
out of the womb I sanctified thee, and I
ORDAINED THEE a prophet unto
the nations."*

Jeremiah 1:5

Abortion

"And the LORD GOD formed man of the dust of the ground, and BREATHED into his nostrils the BREATH OF LIFE; and man became a living soul."
Genesis 2:7

G od is the author of life. He is the One who gives man the ability to breathe, think, eat, and operate. Acts 17:25 says, *"He giveth to all life, and breath, and all things...."* God does not give life to an individual the moment he leaves his mother's womb. No, life begins at the moment of conception.

Nowhere in the Bible does God ever refer to an unborn child as simply a fetus. In fact, in Ecclesiastes 11:5 we read:

> *"As thou knowest not what is the way of the spirit, nor how the bones do grow in the womb of her that is WITH CHILD even so thou knowest not the works of God who maketh all."*

Clearly, God takes credit for the formation of a child, a human being, referring to it as His own work (a work of

God). Notice also that He refers to the unborn as a "child" and not a "fetus." God's Word teaches us that once a child is conceived in its mother's womb, that child is the fulfillment of God's plan for the creation of life. It is a living, human being. Before that child inside that womb is ever given a name, it has a calling from God.

One of the greatest examples of this is found in Isaiah 49, which speaks of Jesus and the fact that God assigned a mission for His life while He was still in the womb of His mother, Mary.

> *"Listen, O isles, unto me; and hearken, ye people, from far; The LORD hath called me from the womb; from the bowels of my mother hath he made mention of my name"* (Isaiah 49:1).

In today's society, Mary would likely be faced with tremendous criticism. She was not married and was engaged to a man who was not the father of her unborn baby. Faced with that situation today, the consensus would be that Mary should get an abortion. Today's society would have encouraged Mary to abort Jesus! Think about it for a moment. What would this world be like today if that had happened?

Well, it does happen today. Many in our society feel that a woman's right to choose supercedes a child's right to live, and our government, as an entity, agrees.

But what does the Bible say? As is recorded in Matthew's Gospel, God has a very serious viewpoint concerning the treatment of His children. He makes that perfectly clear in Matthew 18:6, where He cautioned against offending His children.

> *"But whoso shall offend one of these little ones which believe in me, it were better for him that a millstone were hanged about his neck, and [that] he were drowned in the depth of the sea" (Matthew 18:6).*

In the Old Testament, punishment for one who was responsible for the death of an unborn child was death (Exodus 21:22).

Abortion is wrong. It is as much an act of murder as taking a gun and shooting someone. It is clearly Satan's agenda manifested in the earth.

Seeing that the Word of God says in Ephesians 5:11 that we are to have no fellowship with the unfruitful works of darkness, Christians have no place endorsing Satan's agenda by voting for those who will support it. Jesus wouldn't.

How would Jesus vote on the issue of abortion?

☐ Yes ☑ No

"For this cause God gave them up unto VILE AFFECTIONS: for even their women did change the NATURAL USE into that which is AGAINST NATURE: And likewise also the men, leaving the NATURAL USE of the woman, burned in their lust one toward another; MEN WITH MEN working that which is UNSEEMLY, and receiving in themselves that recompence of their error which was meet."

Romans 1:26, 27

Same Sex Marriage

"Thou shalt not lie with mankind as with womankind:
it is ABOMINATION."
Leviticus 18:22

H omosexual behavior is an abomination before God, Whose viewpoint concerning the issue is simple—it is sin. It is just as much sin as adultery, fornication, stealing, or murder (and is often grouped with these sins in the Bible). However, while God totally destroyed the cities of Sodom and Gomorrah because of the serious epidemic of homosexuality that existed there, He never destroyed an entire city because of the presence of adultery, fornication, stealing or murder. This should tell us something about God's feelings where homosexual behavior is concerned.

The Bible says that homosexuality had become so rampant in Sodom that when two angels appeared at Lot's home, every man in the city came to Lot's door asking that he send them out so that they could sleep with them. When Lot offered them his four daughters, who were all virgins, the men refused. They were so caught up in their homosexual affinities that they rejected the companionship of women to have men instead. How twisted can the mind be? God called the sin in that city and in Gomorrah "grievous" (Genesis 18:20), and because of their refusal to repent, allowed His judgment to fall on them.

Why is God so against homosexuality? For the same reason He is against all sin. It leads to death.

"For the wages of sin is death; but the gift of
God is eternal life through Jesus Christ
our Lord" (Romans 6:23).

That scripture is not just talking about natural death, although that, too, is a by-product of this sin. Romans 1:27 and 1 Corinthians 6:18 support the fact that the ills of homosexual behavior manifest in other areas, such as spiritual death, sickness, poverty, depression, family break-ups and more. Ultimately, it allows Satan to have his destructive way in the lives of the very people Jesus shed His blood to save.

Understand that God hates the sin of homosexuality, but He loves the homosexual (and He expects His children to walk in love with them as well). He wants them to receive His Son, Jesus, and have eternal life with all of its benefits. Homosexuality is just another trap that Satan uses to kill, steal, and destroy; thus, causing more people to spend eternity in hell with him.

There are those who sincerely believe that God is responsible for the existence of homosexuals. But nowhere in the Bible is there scripture to support such an insane belief. God has never created a person to be a homosexual and since the Bible declares that He does not change (Malachi 3:6), we can be sure that He is not about to start now. Besides, it would be unjust for God to create some as homosexual and then issue such a stern instruction as the one given to Israel in Leviticus 20:13:

> *"If a man also lie with mankind, as he lieth with a woman, both of them have committed an abomination: they shall surely be put to death; their blood shall be upon them."*

Homosexuality is a choice, and Satan has deceived many into choosing it as a lifestyle. The Bible prophesies that it will get worse because the anti-Christ is considered to be homosexual. (See Daniel 11:37.)

In recent times, the subject of homosexuality has become very prominent in our society. Where it was once considered shameful to mention the subject, it has become so high profile that even television programs focus on it. In some cases, the entire theme of some television programs is centered on the subject of gays and lesbians.

Because of unwise decision-making by those who serve on the Supreme Court, the election of many who champion unholy beliefs concerning the issue, and the blatant rejection of the Word of God by many churches and some whole denominations, the homosexual lifestyle is rapidly becoming accepted in society. This has led to a push for the acceptance of such things as same sex marriages and the right for homosexual couples to adopt and raise children (both concepts stand in stark contrast to God's position on the subject). Little by little, our country is taking on the image of a Sodom or a Gomorrah.

Those of us with young children must prepare ourselves for the fact that when our children go to school, they may be taught by homosexual teachers, have homosexual coaches, pal around with homosexual classmates, or have classmates whose parents are homosexual. I personally know of an established group of lesbians in my own hometown who start recruiting new members when they are nine years old.

As Christians we must recognize the attack of the enemy on our country and purpose to stand on God's principles no matter how unpopular it may make us. Jesus said they hated Him and that they would hate us (John 15:18, 19).

The Word of God teaches us to hate evil (Proverbs 8:13), not support it. Many choose to support what they know is wrong simply because they fear what may happen to them otherwise, especially where their finances are concerned. It is amazing the impact fear has on someone when it comes to making a choice with regard to standing on God's Word. They fail to realize that the nation's economy is not dependent on any particular policy, but on its moral stand. (See Isaiah 1:4,7.) America is a great country because America is good. That is how we received our prosperity—a prosperity that is above that of the rest of the world. It is because our morality has always been above nations. Sadly, that is in great jeopardy.

Jesus never condoned sin in any form, and neither should we. By choosing not to elect those whose values accept and support homosexuality and same sex marriage, we follow Jesus' example.

How would Jesus vote on the issue of allowing same sex marriages and parenting in our country?

 Yes  No

"For even when we were with you, this we commanded you, that if ANY WOULD NOT WORK, neither should he eat."

2 Thessalonians 3:10

Welfare: Helping the Needy

"He that hath PITY UPON THE POOR lendeth unto the Lord; and that which HE HATH GIVEN will he pay him again."
Proverbs 19:17

God's viewpoint concerning the poor is clear: He loves them and cares about their well being. That is why throughout the Bible He repeatedly reminds His people of their responsibility before Him to give to the poor.

Jesus obeyed this command. Throughout the gospels, we find that an abundance of money came in to support Jesus and His disciples as they spread the good news of the kingdom of God. It was Jesus' practice to use a portion of this money for the support of the poor. He even assigned a treasurer, Judas Iscariot, as keeper and distributor of the funds. (See John 13:29.)

Through His generosity, Jesus illustrated to those who followed Him that the poor are always on God's mind and should be taken care of. The lesson for the church is that if the poor were always on God's mind, then we should be thinking of them also. *"The righteous considereth the cause of the poor: [but] the wicked regardeth not to know it" (Proverbs 29:7.)*

A righteous government is one that will consider the cause of the poor. It is this type of government that God blesses. It is a government that ultimately prospers. As believers, our goal should be to make sure that those placed into government would consider the cause of the poor.

In fairness, we must make certain that those we deem to be poor are, indeed, in need. God never intended that the poor man be sustained by the kindness of others, while he makes no effort to better himself. He is not to spend his life lying prostrate on his back, having grapes dropped ceremoniously into his mouth by those who have chosen to work hard enough to get their own grapes.

No, God's position on laziness is made quite clear in the Bible:

> *"For even when we were with you, this we commanded you, that if any would not work, neither should he eat" (2 Thessalonians 3:10).*

In 1 Thessalonians 4, the Apostle Paul writes that man should work with his hands so that he will have lack of nothing, (See verse 12.) In Proverbs 10:4, we read: *"He becometh poor that dealeth with a slack hand: but the hand of the diligent maketh rich."*

Further, the Scripture reveals that man has a responsibility before God to *"look well to thy herds,"* meaning he must do whatever is necessary (within God's guidelines, of course) to make sure he and his family are financially healthy (Proverbs 27:23).

Jesus showed us in Matthew 11:5 that money is not always the answer to the poor man's problem.

> *"The blind receive their sight, and the lame walk, the lepers are cleansed, and the deaf hear, the dead are raised up, and the poor have the gospel preached to them"* *(Matthews 11:5).*

The biggest problem for a poor person is not that he or she lacks money. It's that they lack the knowledge, discipline, and diligence to obtain money, and the wisdom to use it properly. We, as Christians, and we as a nation do a disservice to the poor when we attempt to solve their problems with money only. Surely, we should help them financially, but we should also make an effort to show them how to climb out of the pit of poverty. We should give them the information they need, both natural and spiritual, that will ultimately cause them to be successful. In other words, don't just give the man a fish, teach the man to fish so he can get his own fish everyday.

The problem with some of our government programs today is that they encourage and reward laziness. They lend credence to the argument that "Because I am here on planet Earth, I am entitled to financial support whether I work at all." It breeds a victim mentality versus a victor mentality.

Yes, there are some who truly need and should receive government support in its present form (grown and able men should not). But for those who should not, we need a work/reward system that requires a certain level of behavior and diligence from its participants. We need to focus on helping people get back on their feet, not supporting them as they lay around on their backs.

Yes, we as Christians, and our government should help the poor, but we should also point them in the proper direction for their lives so they can eventually provide for themselves.

How would Jesus vote on the issue of helping the needy?

"For I say unto you, That unto EVERY ONE WHICH HATH shall be GIVEN; and from him that hath not, even that he hath shall be taken away from him."

Luke 19:26

Taxes and the Economy

"Bring ye all THE TITHES into the storehouse, that there may be meat in mine house..."
Malachi 3:10

---

od's tax code is simple. It's a flat tax called "the tithe." The word *tithe* means "tenth." God requires that those in His Kingdom return to Him one tenth or ten percent of their income—whether they are wealthy or not.

In the Book of Leviticus, God makes it clear that He considers the tithe to belong to Him: *"And all the tithe of the land, [whether] of the seed of the land, [or] of the fruit of the tree, is the LORD'S: [it is] holy unto the LORD" (Leviticus 27:30)*. And in Proverbs 3:9, God refers to the tithe as the "first fruits." He expects the tenth to be taken out before any portion of the income is spent or used.

The tithe is one of the resources used to help fulfill God's purpose for the church, or His Kingdom. That includes the teaching and preaching of the gospel, providing for those in ministry, and seeing after the needs of the underprivileged in society. God requires that everyone who is a part of the body of Christ, regardless of their income, return the tithe to Him.

The interesting thing is that, being a God of integrity, He does not require more than the tithe from one person while requesting only the tithe from the other. He does not penalize His people who are more successful than others by requiring them to pay a higher amount just because they make more money. Actually, in God's kingdom the wealthy that live according to God's law and are tithers and givers only become wealthier.

In Luke 19 we read the parable of the pound, which Jesus prefaces by stating that this is how God's kingdom operates (See Matthew 25:14). The parable relates that the master (representing God) was pleased by those who took the pounds he gave them and produced more pounds, and that he was displeased with the one who did not produce for him. In the midst of judging the unprofitable servant, the master says, *"Take from him the pound, and give it to him that hath ten pounds" (Luke 19:24)*. His servants remarked to him that this man had ten pounds already, thinking that he should give it to the individual with five pounds so that they would be closer to even, a viewpoint that many have today, but one that God does not share. (God is not a socialist!)

The master further states, "To him that hath shall be given." Why would he say that? God rewards diligence. He set up this planet and His kingdom so that the diligent would prosper and those who were not diligent would not (See Proverbs 10:4). In the parable, God did not take from the richer servant because he happened to be rich and the other happened to not be so rich. He actually took from the poor and gave to the rich because the rich knew how to properly use what he had. The poor did not exercise sound wisdom in the use of the pound he had been given.

This is not to say that God hates the poor or that He is going to start taking their money tomorrow and giving it to the rich; nor is it to say that our government should do so. It is only to point out to you that God rewards creativity, diligence, and effort. He does not raise His tax rate to account for every income bracket, and thereby penalize a person by taking more of his money because he had enough discipline and diligence to obtain it. (Imagine what it would be like if the tax principle of today were applied in our school systems. So that things would be fair, we would take the A that a student made on a test and give it to the student whose grade was a C.)

What God has given every person the opportunity to choose his or her own direction in life. Those who do well and those who do not do well are required to return to him the same percentage of their increase. Jesus would support those who pattern our economic plan after the most successful one ever created—God's plan. And so should we.

How would Jesus vote on the issue of a flat tax?

 **Yes** ☐ **No**

"For GOD SO LOVED the World that he gave his only begotten Son that WHOSOEVER believeth in him should not perish, but have EVERLASTING LIFE.."

John 3:16

Freedom of Religion:
Separation of Church and State

"And THIS GOSPEL of the kingdom shall be preached IN
ALL THE WORLD for a witness unto all nations..."
Matthew 24:14

God's number one goal is for His gospel to be spread all across the world so that every man, woman, boy, and girl can have the opportunity to receive His Son, Jesus, and have everlasting life. This is why Jesus came to the earth in the first place—to "seek and save the lost" (Luke 19:10). He came to the planet, endured a brutal death at the hands of man, went to hell for three days and nights, and was resurrected so that man would have the opportunity to hear the good news and be "born again" into His Father's kingdom.

To Him and His Father, the best political atmosphere is one in which the gospel can be preached freely. This is illustrated by 1 Timothy 2:1–4, where Paul exhorts Timothy to pray for those in authority or positions of influence, so that we may lead a quiet and peaceable life (actually God is also speaking to the believer). Whether you like it or not, this includes politicians, your bosses, and anyone who is over you.

In verse 4, we see why it is so important that we pray for these individuals and that we live in a peaceful atmosphere: *"Who will have all men to be saved, and to come unto the knowledge of the truth" (1 Timothy 2:4).*

We see in the Book of Acts what happened when the early church did this.

> *"Then had the churches rest throughout all Judaea and Galilee and Samaria, and were edified; and walking in the fear of the Lord, and in the comfort of the Holy Ghost, were multiplied" (Acts 9:31).*

Recently, this mission has come under attack in a number of ways beginning with the false argument propagated by those who oppose God concerning the separation of church and state. This argument is rooted in the belief that there is no place for God in public society and government, therefore nothing that represents or makes reference to Him should be allowed in those arenas. One of the recent results of this movement is a court ruling that states the words under God should be removed from our Pledge of Allegiance. Another is the removal of the Ten Commandments from government buildings, despite the fact that this country was founded on these principles. The proponents of this argument falsely state that this is a constitutional argument. Nothing could be further from the truth.

The phrase "separation of church and state" is not found anywhere in the Constitution or its First Amendment. In fact, it is not found in any of our official government documents of that time. The First Amendment reads in part: "Congress shall make no law respecting an establishment or religion, or prohibiting the free exercise thereof...." Its main purpose was to protect churches from the state more so than the state from the church. However, many liberals have taken this amendment out of its historical context and distorted its meaning to advance their ungodly ideas of what America should be while branding any other type of thinking, particularly Christian, as extremist.

In addition to the overt attack on the things of God in politics today, it is interesting that government has no problem sticking its nose into the business of the church. During the late nineties in Washington and other parts of the country, a number of laws were passed that ultimately harmed the church, and ministries as a whole. One example is the government limiting the amount of income a minister can make—no matter how many lives his ministry touches. This is something that the government does not do to any other profession, not even to the largest purveyors of pornography in our country. All the while, many Christians are blindly voting for and loyal to the same individuals who have been hindering their churches from growing and expanding. All in all, our governmental institutions are making it harder for the body of Christ to preach the gospel.

The Great Commission came from the very mouth of Jesus. Surely, He would not vote for those who would position themselves to stop it from coming to pass. As Christians, our number one priority should be the preaching of the gospel and we should in no way support those who would stand in the way of our doing so.

How would Jesus vote with regard to freedom of religion?

 ☑Yes ☐No

*"Where there is neither Greek nor Jew,
circumcision nor uncircumcision,
Barbarian, Scythian, bond nor free: but
Christ is all, and in all."*

Colossians 3:11

Racism

"For there is no difference between the Jew and the Greek: for the same Lord over all is rich unto all that call upon him."
Romans 10:12

G od hates racism. Why? Racism, or prejudice, is a manifestation of hatred and God is not a God of hatred. He is a God of love.

Racism is a tool of Satan, the mortal enemy of God. Satan uses racism to divide and conquer the inhabitants of the earth—the same inhabitants God sent His Son to die for. Indeed, Genesis 12:3 shows us the plan of God from near the beginning concerning Jesus: *"in thee shall ALL FAMILIES of the earth be blessed."*

God sent His Son, Jesus, to die for all mankind, not just for those of a particular race. When He paid the ultimate price for mankind, He placed the same value on every man, woman, boy, and girl. Skin color had nothing what-soever to do with that price, which was the blood of Jesus Christ. As far as God is concerned, man is man. In His eyesight, there is no white, black, or yellow man. All men are, in fact, created equal. The only color that really matters to God is red—the color that signifies you have been washed in the blood.

As Romans 3 teaches us, all have sinned. Therefore, all can be made righteous before God. The only separation God makes between men is based on whether they have accepted His Son, Jesus. They are either righteous and therefore on His side, or they are unrighteous and standing against Him, alongside the enemy.

Even though God does not like unbelief, His love for mankind is so great that He does not instruct the righteous to hate the unrighteous. No, we are to love them with the love of God and share the gospel of Jesus Christ with them.

The ultimate example of God's "color-blindness," is found in the Book of Numbers, Chapter 12. There, we find that Moses married an Ethiopian woman and it angered his brother, Aaron, and his sister, Miriam. Why? Because she was of a different skin color than they.

God came down in a cloud and dealt directly with Aaron and Miriam, forcefully correcting them for speaking against Moses. Not once did God mention the fact that Moses had taken an Ethiopian woman as his wife. Why? It was not an issue with God. He continued to deal with Moses as He always had. Moses had done nothing wrong.

My point here is simple. Racism is not of God, but of the devil. Therefore, it is something to be opposed; not only in our own lives, but also in our churches and our government. We should not be party to electing those who would side with Satan on this issue and implement policies that are designed to limit or hurt people of another race, color, or nationality. To do so is to be involved in the very thing Jesus came to free us from—hatred. It also positions us to receive the negative eternal consequences as well.

We should always vote for those who love all men and will serve with the good of all men in mind. Jesus was the ultimate example of this. He surely would not vote for someone who would not follow His example.

How would Jesus vote on the issue of racism?

 Yes  No

*"And ye shall TEACH THEM (HIS WORDS)
YOUR CHILDREN, speaking
of them when thou sittest in thine house,
and when thou walkest by the way, when
thou liest down, and when thou
risest up."*

Deuteronomy 11:19

Education:
Prayer in the Schools

"But whoso shall offend one of these LITTLE ONES which believe in me, it were better for him that a millstone were hanged about his neck, and that he were drowned in the depth of the sea."
Matthew 18:6

God loves His little ones, and He has a very serious viewpoint concerning them and those who would harm them. When God says it would be better to drown with a millstone around your neck than to have to face Him for offending one of His little ones, that tells me just how serious He is about the matter. The Word teaches about God's desire for godly seed and His desire for His children to be brought up in such a way that they become mighty in the earth just like Him.

Jesus would receive little children brought to Him and lay His hands on them, endowing them with power so they could be prosperous. God's Word shows us in Deuteronomy 11 and Ephesians 6 that He desires for it to be "well with them" and for them to have "days of heaven on the earth." Scripture after scripture supports God's concern for His children, showing just how important they and everything pertaining to them are to Him.

Just as God makes His wisdom available to us as His children so we can make right and righteous decisions, providing our children with a good education should be a priority with us. Our children are our future and the education we give them now will determine where our country ends up later.

The major issue with our school system is the government-forced removal of God from our schools. If you add to that the government-endorsed introduction of the "religion" called Humanism, which is being forced on our children, then you can see why evils like teen pregnancy and violence have increased greatly in our schools.

Today's children are being taught that creation is a fable and evolution is science; that morals are situational, but homosexuality is normal. Our universities have become nothing more than breeding grounds that take balanced, God-fearing children and make them candidates for an eternal ticket to hell by turning them into opponents of God, His ways, and His purpose. Prayer has been taken out of school; not only prayer, but also God Himself.

Jesus, a man of prayer, would elect God-fearing men and women to our courts who would reverse the current trends in our educational system. He would vote for those who would make a way for children to be trained in the things of God— not just at home, but in our schools. We need to do the same.

How would Jesus vote on the issue of good education
and prayer in our schools?

 Yes ☐ No

*"Thus saith the Lord; Execute ye judgment
and righteousness, and deliver the spoiled
out of the hand of the oppressor: and DO
NO WRONG, DO NO VIOLENCE TO THE
STRANGER, the fatherless, nor the widow,
neither shed innocent blood
in this place."*

Jeremiah 22:3

Israel and the Promised Land

"And the Lord appeared unto Abram, and said, Unto THY
SEED will I GIVE THIS LAND: and there builded he an
altar unto the Lord, who appeared unto him."
Genesis 12:7

The Book of Genesis reveals a wonderful relationship between God and Abram (later called Abraham), and the promises God made to this man who would become known as the father of the nation of Israel. Among other things, God promised to give Abram and his seed the land of Canaan, an area that we know includes present-day Israel as well as parts of other nations.

Although it belonged to others, God awarded this land to Abram by promise because of the sin of the people (Canaan was a land of grievous sin). Over time, and with the help of Jehovah, Israel conquered all of the land that was promised to them (See Joshua 21:43–45). However, Israel soon fell into a pattern of falling into sin, the same as the Canaanites before them, and lost the land God had given them. The Book of Jeremiah (16:15, 29:14) shows us that while they were in captivity, God promised that He would restore them to their land once again (a promise repeated in other books of the Bible as well). That promise was partly fulfilled after almost two thousand years when in the late 1940s Israel became a nation again.

> *"But, The LORD liveth, that brought up the children of Israel from the land of the north, and from all the lands whither he had driven them: and I will bring them again into their land that I gave unto their fathers"* (Jeremiah 16:15).

> *"And I will be found of you, saith the LORD: and I will turn away your captivity, and I will gather you from all the nations, and from all the places whither I have driven you, saith the LORD; and I will bring you again into the place whence I caused you to be carried away captive"* (Jeremiah 29:14).

As far as God is concerned, the land of Israel belongs to Israel—all of it. As believers we need to agree with God versus the latest political trend or belief and support Israel's efforts to protect their God-given land. The Bible teaches that God will bless those that bless Israel and that we, as believers, should pray for peace in Jerusalem. The point is clear. As Christians, we are to be on Israel's side as a nation. Up until now, our nation has offered our support to Israel and has been greatly blessed as a result.

Although all of the land is Israel's, God does require Israel to operate according to His principles concerning the strangers in their land, including those who do not serve their God. God requires that they do no violence to them or wrong them. Deuteronomy 14 goes so far as to say that one of the purposes for the tithe in that time was to provide help for "the stranger" in the land. The strangers, in this case, are the Palestinians. Israel has a right to protect itself from terrorist attack or any other threat against their people, but they do not have a right to arbitrarily destroy the homes of and displace the Palestinian people.

Jesus would vote according to His Fathers' plan and not the plan of man. He would vote so that Israel would be able to keep its land, but also be encouraged not to do wrong to the stranger in their land. We should follow this example and vote for those who will push for God's agenda in the land of Israel.

How would Jesus vote regarding peace in Jerusalem?

 ☑Yes ☐No

"THE HORSE IS PREPARED against the DAY OF BATTLE: but safety is of the Lord."

Proverbs 21:31

ISSUE NO. 9

War and National Defense

"Thou shalt not KILL."
Exodus 20:13

T here are those who say that war, in any form,
is wrong and that it is sin. And they use the
scripture recorded in Exodus 20:13 to support
their claim.

However, they fail to understand that the original
Hebrew word *kill* as it is used in this context literally
means "to murder." They also fail to recognize that many
times in the Old Testament, God commanded Israel to go
to war against its enemies (and not just for defensive
purposes), and that He fought alongside them (See Joshua
10:11). In the New Testament, it is clearly stated that when
Jesus returns, He and His army will defeat a large gath-
ering of armies at Armageddon and that His victory will be
so great that blood will rise unto the horses' bridle.

There are times, in God's eyes, when war is right and
necessary. That is not to say that we should be warmon-

gers, looking for the opportunity to fight. But it is to say that we as a nation should be sensitive to the direction of God and support our country, especially our soldiers, in the time of war.

> *"A time to love, and a time to hate; a time of war, and a time of peace" (Ecclesiastes 3:8).*

When David was confronted with the issue of his nation going to war, not only did he support his people, but God anointed him to fight and win a great victory over Goliath and the Philistines (1 Samuel 17:37, 50–52). Clearly, there is a "time to war"—a time when God says to do so.

Another biblical principle pertaining to war and national defense is found in Proverbs 21:31. It shows us that as a nation, we must always be prepared in the event of war, even though our safety is of the Lord. With God, you must do the natural and He will provide the super-natural. You must do your part, and then He will do His part. As a nation that serves God, our part is to make sure that our military is fully prepared to face any situation. In the Bible, Israel was constantly faced with such situations and many times had an army trained, ready to fight even if they ultimately needed God's help to win. (See 2 Chronicles 20.)

Jesus would vote for those who fully understand this principle and apply it by making sure our nation has a strong military and is led by God in our decisions to go to war.

How would Jesus vote on the issue of national defense?

"When the RIGHTEOUS ARE IN AUTHORITY, the PEOPLE REJOICE: but when the wicked beareth rule, the people mourn."

Proverbs 29:2

Christians in Politics

"Having then GIFTS DIFFERING according to the GRACE that is given to us... he that RULETH with diligence..."
Romans 12:6, 8

God calls and anoints people in His kingdom to be in the political arena and to be a major influence over millions by their service in government. His objective for them is to rule according to His principles with the help of His power. His desired result is that the people they rule over prosper and rejoice. Indeed, Proverbs 29:2 shows us that when those that are righteous are placed in positions of authority, and they continue to act righteously in these positions (which is implied in the scripture), the people rejoice. There should be, and recognizably so, a big difference in the effect on a nation when the righteous rule versus the rule of the wicked. This is very important for Christians to consider.

In 1 Timothy 2:1–4, God instructs Christians to pray for kings and those in authority. He does so because of the overarching reach and the lasting effects of these leaders' decision-making power. Their decisions can lead to life for some and death for others. They can lead to war or peace, bring about prosperity or poverty, endorse sin and death or encourage righteousness and life. What better people to have in these positions of authority than God's people? People who know God, love God, and live according to His Word will bring about the results He desires and that we desire in our country today.

Many hours of prayer devoted to asking God to touch the hearts of and change the decisions and policy stances of unbelievers in positions of authority (many who are put there by believers in the name of money, race, or more) can be replaced by hours of prayer spent upholding those who are righteous. Instead of praying for the country to not be torn down, we can pray that it be upheld because the righteous in authority have put it in a position to prosper. (That is how this great country became great in the first place.)

Some say there is no place for God-fearing people, Christians, in government. First of all, ignore the non-Christian who says so. He knows nothing of God or His ways, and therefore is in no position to pass judgment on what is appropriate for a Christian. The non-Christian would force his secular views on you, but negate your right to voice your Christian viewpoint.

Secondly, for those who are Christians and say so, I want to point to the Word of God on the issue.

Melchizedek was a priest of God and a king, as was David a prophet and a king. Both reigned very successfully. Jehoshaphat was a great king, as was Uzziah (until his personal demise due to turning from God), Josiah, Hezekiah, Solomon, and many more. All of these men caused their nation, and therefore their people, to prosper. During Solomon's reign, the nation was so prosperous, he gave silver to the people in abundance (See 1 Kings 10).

And how about Jesus? The Bible teaches that He will reign on earth for a thousand years and that it will be the most prosperous thousand years that man has ever experienced. He's not doing a bad job reigning over His spiritual kingdom now, providing for every need of His citizens.

My point is simple. God anointed men to be in government and in authority. When they obeyed Him, while in those positions, they and their people prospered.

That principle still holds true today, God still anoints men to rule, and if they will seek Him in the process of doing so, they will find that the people under their authority will rejoice as well. Think about it, what better person to have in Washington than a man or woman who has God's ear and who receives wisdom concerning even difficult situations from the throne room itself—someone like Solomon or Moses? This is ultimately the will of God, which is why He calls and anoints some to do it.

There may be some who like to play the "religion card" and say they are born-again. But remember, the Bible says you will know them by their fruit. That does not mean they will never make mistakes, but they need to have genuinely accepted Jesus into their hearts and have lives that reflect that they are born-again Christians.

> *"That if thou shalt confess with thy mouth the Lord Jesus, and shalt believe in thine heart that God hath raised him from the dead, thou shalt be saved. For with the heart man believeth unto righteousness; and with the mouth confession is made unto salvation"* *(Romans 10:9–10).*

Jesus would get involved in politics, if called to by God (and remember, He is) and would vote for the righteous who will rule according to God's Word and principles, and so should we.

How would Jesus vote regarding Christian participation in the political arena?

Conclusion

"Be ye therefore imitators of God, as beloved children."
(Ephesians 5:1 American Standard Version)

I f Jesus were a United States citizen with all the legal rights and responsibilities of voting, He would vote according to God's Word. He would not be swayed by the economy, the media, the current popular opinion, or what is seemingly politically correct. He would not sit back on the sidelines and not vote, or throw up His hands in disgust when it appeared that immorality was winning. Jesus would exercise His right to vote and He would vote according to God's Word.

In Ephesians 5:1, the Bible instructs us to be imitators of God. As imitators of God, we are required to imitate Jesus. We must, therefore, look at today's political issues the same way Jesus would. We must not be swayed by the economy, the media, the current popular opinion, or what is seemingly politically correct. We must not sit back on the sidelines and not vote, or throw up our hands in disgust when it appears that immorality is winning. No, we must imitate Jesus. We must exercise our right to vote, and we must vote according to God's Word.

The KingdomHasCome, LLC
"Building God's Kingdom One Soul At A Time"

The vision of The KingdomHasCome, LLC is to spread the good news of the gospel of Jesus Christ by creating products that will minister God's Word and His love to the hearts and minds of people in a practical and creative way in order to reach the world for Jesus Christ.